Ronald Knox

by
Fr Ashley Beck

*All booklets are published thanks to the
generous support of the members of the
Catholic Truth Society*

CATHOLIC TRUTH SOCIETY
PUBLISHERS TO THE HOLY SEE

Contents

Acknowledgements

My first debt of gratitude is to my old school, King Edward VI School, Southampton. In spite of its Protestant foundation, it was there that I first encountered Ronald Knox's books (and one of the books written by his brother Wilfred) nearly forty years ago; I am also grateful to my wife Caroline who has over the years bought me many of them from second hand bookshops, and to Mary and Mervyn Shipsey. Finally, I am once more grateful to the staff and pupils of St Mary's School, Beckenham, for affording me time during our school journey to Hayling Island in Hampshire in May 2008 to write much of this booklet; Knox would have been a much more entertaining and edifying chaplain.

A true apologist

From time to time very definite written attacks are launched on the Christian faith, of varying degrees of intellectual depth, either through clear criticism or by means of a more subtle medium such as a novel or a film. Examples would include recent works by Richard Dawkins and Dan Brown. Catholics need to be able to respond with calm confidence to such attacks and give a reasonable and convincing account of their faith: this is the art known as *apologetics*. In England one of the great masters of this art in the 20th century was Monsignor Ronald Knox, writer, translator of the Scriptures and Catholic Chaplain at Oxford. Just over fifty years after his death this booklet attempts to give a picture of his life and the abiding importance of his writings.

I first encountered Knox in a school library in the early 1970s. This was through one of his most popular books, *The Mass in Slow Motion*, sermons about the Mass originally preached during the Second World War to girls from the Assumption Convent School in Kensington who had been evacuated to Aldenham in Shropshire, where Knox was engaged in his translation of the Bible. Knox's ability to combine sure-footed doctrine with an easy way of understanding young minds is one of the most striking and attractive aspects of that book (and of its companion volumes *The Creed in Slow Motion* and *The Gospel in Slow Motion*): not without humour, but focussed clearly on how he was trying to explain the different parts of the rite of the Mass to his young charges. It is that talent for explanation and argument which made Knox one of the foremost writers of the first half of the twentieth century, a man whose mastery of English would have made him distinguished in any literary field (indeed, he wrote detective stories as well as books about religion). His explanation of the Christian faith is also rooted in one important concept, now as then: the nature of authority. In the present-day deep divisions among Christians - both between communities and within them - the fundamental issue of dispute is authority. How do we know who teaches the truth? This was the determining factor in his conversion to Catholicism in 1917, as it has been for many others in similar positions (the present writer included) and dominated his writings after that.

It should not be thought that because he is a figure from pre-conciliar Catholicism he has nothing to say to twenty-first century Catholics, or that interest in him is a sign of reactionary nostalgia: on the contrary, his ability to explain the message of Catholicism in everyday language, his passionate search for truth, his commitment to the notion of authority, his deep love for the Mass, his profound knowledge of the Bible, all make him a figure of abiding and contemporary importance; his opinions on a variety of topics mean that he cannot be easily pigeonholed. He remains important culturally and ecumenically: he appears in Howard Brenton's 2008 play about Macmillan, *Never So Good*, and the Archbishop of Canterbury, Dr Rowan Williams, quoted him in a speech to the Anglican General Synod in February 2008, something which in itself would have amused him.[1]

In recent years some of his works have been reprinted, and in the United States there is a *Ronald Knox Society*, so this is a good time to reawaken interest in him in England.

Early life and ministry in the Church of England

Childhood

Ronald Arbuthnott Knox was born on 17th February 1888 in Kibworth, Leicestershire into an Anglican family and environment. His parents were Edmund Knox, at that time Rector of the Anglican parish of Kibworth, and Ellen Knox, daughter of Bishop Thomas French. Edmund Knox was one of the most influential figures in the Evangelical movement in the Church of England, becoming Suffragan Bishop of Coventry (within the diocese of Lichfield), a post he combined with being Archdeacon and Rector of the vast parish of Aston in Birmingham, and from 1903 until 1921 Bishop of Manchester. Of Knox's siblings most led distinguished lives: his oldest brother Edmund (known as 'Evoe') was a noted poet and writer, and became a very successful editor of *Punch*; his older sister Winifred, later Lady Peck, was also a writer; his brother Dillwyn was a distinguished classicist and Fellow of King's College, Cambridge, involved also in intelligence and code-breaking work in both world wars; and his younger brother Wilfred became an influential Anglican clergyman

and writer and towards the end of his life Chaplain of
Pembroke College, Cambridge.[2] Their mother died of
influenza in 1892. In 1895, just after being made a bishop,
Edmund Knox married again; his new wife Ethel was the
daughter of Canon Newton, Vicar of Redditch.

Ronald was thus surrounded in his family by men
distinguished in the active ministry of the established
Church; we should also remember that at the end of the
Victorian age the Anglican Church was one of the most
important institutions in the whole of the British Empire,
at the heart of its corporate life and of its ruling class. For
anyone in such a family to walk away from this and
become a Roman Catholic was a far bigger step than it
might be today.

Eton

The family atmosphere in which the children grew up, in
spite of the sad death of their mother, was marked by a
striking sense of *rapport* and intellectual brilliance. After
Bishop Knox's remarriage, in spite of his objection to
boarding schools, the boys were destined for major public
schools: Edmund and Wilfred going to Rugby, Dillwyn
and Ronald to Eton. He entered that most famous of
English schools in September 1900 and his time in the
school remained the most formative influence on his life
and in some ways the place where he was happiest. Its
history dating back to the middle Ages entranced him;

this helped to form his early devotion to the Mother of God and to the saintly King Henry VI who had dedicated his foundation to her. It was also the environment in which his genius for writing and wit first flourished, coupled with his deep and brilliant expertise in Latin. He duly became 'Captain of the School' (Head Boy) and edited or founded a number of journals such as the *Eton Chronicle* and *The Outsider*; also towards the end of his time at the school he published his first book, *Signa Severa*, a collection of English, Latin and Greek verses.

More importantly, his religious faith became much stronger when he was at school: he discovered the 'Anglo-Catholic' tradition. This was an outlook, with its roots in the time of King Charles I in the seventeenth century, and becoming very important after the 'Oxford Movement' in the nineteenth,[3] which saw the Church of England as being in essential respects part of the wider Catholic Church, in spite of having been divided from the rest of western Christendom at the Reformation: the adherents of this tradition held (and still do) that it had retained valid orders and sacraments, and they were passionately committed to ending the breach with Rome. He became a weekly communicant and at the age of seventeen made a vow of celibacy, as he wrote in *A Spiritual Aeneid*: "Conscious for the first time how much my nature craved for human sympathy and support, I thought it my obvious duty to deny myself that tenderest sympathy and support which a happy marriage would bring. I must have 'power to attend upon the Lord without impediment.'" His religious sense was also deepened by a serious bout of appendicitis he suffered just before he left school.

Oxford

He went up to Oxford with a scholarship to Balliol College, in 1906, a college marked by effortless intellectual brilliance and, at that time, internal divisions among the undergraduates. At Balliol the strongest influence on him was the Junior Dean, F. F. ('Sligger') Urquhart, the first Catholic since the Reformation to be elected a Fellow of an Oxford college and Knox's first Catholic friend. At Oxford Knox combined a brilliant academic career in Classics, winning various prestigious prizes, widening his circle of friends beyond men he had known at Eton, and becoming President of the Oxford Union in 1909; throughout his life he was a skilled and witty debater.

His adherence to the 'Anglo-Catholic' movement in the Church of England became much more marked at Oxford. The centre of his devotional life was not Balliol College Chapel but Pusey House and the 'Cowley Fathers', the house of the order of Anglican clergy known as the Society of St John the Evangelists. By the time of his final exams he was sure he was called to be a priest of the Church of England; such was his ability that before these he was offered a tutorial fellowship and the chaplaincy of Trinity College, without the need to train formally for ordination - he was simply expected to devise his own course of studies.

Young clergyman

The next four years, from 1910 until 1914, were Knox's 'golden age' in the Church of England, surrounded by friends and undergraduates in his pastoral care at Oxford, part of a crusading, exciting movement; among these was the future Prime Minister, Harold Macmillan. While his father Bishop Knox welcomed his son's vocation to the ordained ministry (into which his brother Wilfred followed him) he was strongly opposed to his son's views. Bishop Knox, like other clerical members of the family, was a leading member of the Evangelical movement. He saw Ronald and his friends as traitors, bent on destroying the Church of England and undoing the Reformation. As his son became better known, there were many arguments in the Knox household during holidays.

The twin focal points of his writing and preaching were the overall aims of the 'Anglo-Catholic' movement: opposing those trying to move the Church in a different direction, and movements in biblical scholarship characterised at the time as 'modernism'. The most memorable attacks he made were through the medium of satirical writing, which shows his brilliance as a writer. With regard to the first, one of his gems was *Reunion All Round*, a pastiche of Swift satirising Anglicans who wished to overlook theological differences with Nonconformists ('*A Plea for the Inclusion within the Church of England of all Mahometans, Jews, Buddhists, Brahmins, Papists and Atheists, submitted to the consideration of the British Public*'): this was read out loud to the Prime Minister, H. H. Asquith, while bathing. His attack on what he saw as the excesses of 'higher criticism' was twofold: first, the brilliant poem *Absolute and Abitofhell*, written in the style of Dryden (which rapidly became a best-seller) and *Some Loose Stones*. Knox was reacting to the publication of a book called *Foundations* by some of the most prominent scholars in Oxford (including the future Archbishop of Canterbury, William Temple). In the poem we read:

> 'When suave Politeness, temp'ring bigot Zeal
> Corrected "I believe", to "One does feel."'

As Milton Walsh points out[4] *Some Loose Stones* shows the first signs of apologetic themes which would recur in his later writings - the need for authority over and against subjective experience as the basis of revealed religion, and the naturalness of miracles if our starting point for reflection is belief in the divinity of Christ. Throughout these years it would be wrong to think that he did not question his position in the Church of England: on the eve of his ordination in 1910 he wrote to Sligger Urquhart: 'I don't really see my way beyond Anglican orders at present. At the same time I can't feel that the Church of England is an ultimate solution: in 50 years or a hundred I believe we *Romanizers*[5] will either have got the Church or been turned out of it. I may not live to see it, but I hope never to live so long as to cease praying for it.' And he wrote in *Some Loose Stones*, describing the true road of Christian pilgrimage, that it was really '... straight, because it is the simplest way of accomplishing your journey; straight, because the whole business of faith is not picking and choosing your way, or looking out for signposts, but having the pertinacity to follow your nose; straight, because the road is very largely Roman.'

Conversion

Like John Henry Newman and many others, part of Knox's identity and importance lies in his decision to leave all this behind and become a Roman Catholic. In *A Spiritual Aeneid* he writes of how gradual this process was. He writes of 'a random walk I once took in London, when, turn into the alleys as I would, I still found the great campanile of Westminster looming up in front of me, and I felt to myself that it was saying "I'll have you yet."' It is only rarely that conversion takes place as a sudden event: a more gradual process is far more common.

For many in the extreme, 'papalist' end of the Anglo-Catholic movement there were ecclesiastical events in the early years of Knox's ministry which cast doubt on whether this vision of Anglicanism was tenable: the 'Kikuyu incident' in Kenya, where Nonconformists were admitted to Holy Communion by the Anglican authorities, or the conversion to Catholicism of the entire Anglican Cistercian community on Caldey Island in Wales. Those close to Knox wondered if he might 'pope' (as the expression went) for these reasons. However, for him the key event was not an ecclesiastical phenomenon at all, but the storm which engulfed Europe in August

1914, the First World War. While we certainly cannot say that he would not have become a Catholic if the war had not happened, we can say that the war determined how and at what pace the move happened.

The early war years: from Oxford to Shrewsbury

Knox had arranged to have a 'reading party' of his friends and disciples in the summer vacation of 1914 at a country house in Gloucestershire. In the end nobody came, as they 'joined up' after war was declared. Kenneth Mackenzie, who had just come down from Trinity (and one of the first to be killed), wrote to Knox: 'Alas - I fear I shall not be able to come to Stroud owing to this ridiculous war as I have applied for a commission with a view to "keeping" an Armageddon.' When the Michaelmas term started, Knox found Oxford unbearably deserted, as so many students and dons (like his older brother Eddie) had joined the army. For those who had followed his teachings and felt at home in the extreme Anglo-Catholic wing of the Church of England, the war suddenly posed an urgent question - in the face of death, how would they receive the sacraments, since virtually all Anglican army chaplains had a totally incompatible view of the priest's ministry?[6] Two of his circle, Guy Lawrence and Harold Macmillan[7], indicated to him that they would become Roman Catholics to be sure of sacramental ministrations (although Macmillan did not in fact do so), and Knox realised he could not dissuade them, nor did he wish to. If you cannot honestly encourage people to stay in a religious community when they are facing the likelihood of death, how can you still believe in that community at all?

He needed time to think; he had also to come to terms not only with the departure of his friends from Oxford, but of the deaths of nearly all of them in the trenches as the war progressed. He obtained leave of absence from Trinity and went to teach at Shrewsbury public school, filling the place of Evelyn Southwell, a master and friend of his who was fighting in the war (he felt as a clergyman that he was precluded from bearing arms, and after some hesitations clergy were exempted from conscription). He went there to teach Latin and act a housemaster, not to be school chaplain, and in this final period of his Anglican ministry his public religious functions gradually became minimal - his heart was not in it. His time at Shrewsbury is best remembered for word-games he taught the boys and other activities which can only be described as 'pranks' - in many ways it was pure escapism.

Turning point

His process of moving away from the Church of England was gradual and tortuous in many ways, but a key early turning point was in May 1915: 'I went up to London for the morning of St Augustine's Day, to see my brother celebrate for the first time at St Mary's, Graham Street. We had been brought up together, known one another at Oxford as brothers seldom do. It should have been an occasion of the most complete happiness to see him now, a priest administering for the first time the most august mystery of our religion, in the same church, at the same altar, where I had stood in that position three years before, in his presence. And then, suddenly, I saw the other side to the picture. If this doubt, this shadow of a scruple which had grown up in my mind, were justifiable - only suppose it were justifiable, then neither he nor I was a priest, nor was this the Mass, nor was the host the Saving Host; the accessories of the service - the bright vestments, the fresh flowers, the mysterious candle-light, were all settings to a sham jewel; we had been trapped, deceived, betrayed into thinking it all worth while; we had ploughed the sand, fought over a phantom Helen through all these years of conflict. *Nunc alte vulnus adactum* ['Here is my wound driven home at last', Virgil, *Aeneid* x. 850]...'

As part of his process of decision-making he corresponded with friends who were about to go to the western front; more painfully, he corresponded with his father who tried desperately to dissuade him. At one point Bishop Knox made it clear that he would have to resign his See if his son became a Catholic, which in fact he did not do. During this period Ronald also encountered the renowned Jesuit C.C. Martindale, who at their first meeting made it clear that he had to have positive reasons for becoming a Catholic, advice frequently given to converts dissatisfied with their community. In 1916 he left Shrewsbury and took up clerical War Office work in London, staying and helping a little at the church in Graham Street. By the spring of 1917 it was clear to most who knew him that he would convert, but he still wished to take things slowly and make a proper retreat; but at that time he began to 'burn his bridges' by indicating that he did not wish to be re-elected to his fellowship at Trinity.

Farnborough Abbey

In the autumn he made his retreat at Farnborough Abbey in Hampshire and was received into the Catholic Church by the Abbot on 22nd September. Other converts to Catholicism will be able to understand this allegory: 'It was as if I had been a man homeless and needing shelter, who first of all had taken refuge under a shed at the back of an empty house. Then he had found an outhouse unlocked, and felt more cheerfulness and comfort there. Then he had tried a door in the building itself, and, by some art, found a secret spring which let you in at the back door; nightly thenceforward he had visited this back part of the house, more roomy than anything he had yet experienced, and giving, through a little crack, a view into the wide spaces of the house beyond. Then, one night, he had tried the spring, and the door had refused to open. The button could still be pushed, but it was followed by no sound of groaning hinges. Baffled, and unable now to content himself with shed or outhouse, he had wandered round and round the house, looking enviously at the frowning fastnesses. And then he tried the front door, and found that it had been open all the time.'

The Catholic layman

In the initial period after his reception Knox continued working for the War Office. He was clear in his intention to offer himself for the secular priesthood and was accepted for the archdiocese of Westminster by Cardinal Francis Bourne. Like the Anglican authorities seven years before the cardinal did not expect him to train at a seminary but invited him to devise his own course of formation for two years, while living as paying guest at the Oratory in Knightsbridge. Most converts to the Catholic Church, particularly if they have been clergy, need a quiet period of acclimatisation to accustom themselves to their new communion at various levels: many differences between the Anglican and Catholic communities were more marked in 1917 than they are now, and at his conversion Knox knew very few Catholics. Knox led a quiet life at the Oratory, joining in the community's life; the closing years of the war were marked by the deaths of more friends.

St Edmund's Old Hall - ordination

Given Knox's background in the English public schools and Oxford University, it was natural that the cardinal should choose as a setting for his initial period as a priest St Edmund's Old Hall, Ware, Hertfordshire. This institution, at various times both a public school and a diocesan seminary, was dear to Bourne himself and traced its history back to penal times. In the years following the Great War, the intention was to make it an important public school for Catholics on the same level as the schools run by the religious orders, and someone of Knox's stature was an obvious gain. He wrote in the school magazine many years after he left: 'I came to St Edmund's as a raw recruit, still needing to learn, by contact, the ethos of the Catholic mind.' He was ordained a priest in October 1919 at Westminster.

He was employed to teach Latin at the school and in his time there edited a school edition of some of the books of Virgil's *Aeneid*, a work he knew so well. The standard of education was not high and the place was very disorganised, but like other institutions in which Knox had worked there was ample space for his talents and sense of fun: he was remembered for years afterwards for jumping on a pogo-stick, clad in cassock and biretta. He worked hard to improve the school's standing, especially by recruiting lay masters; he was also part of the plans the cardinal had for restructuring the institution.

Knox the preacher

Very soon after his ordination Knox again was in demand as a preacher, as he had been in his Anglican days. St Edmund's gained prestige from these engagements, which remained a regular feature of his priestly life. He accepted engagements all over the country, fortified by his knowledge of and love for the English railway network. Preaching from a complete written text was not that common among Catholic clergy at that time (nor is it today) but this was always Knox's practice. He kept the typewritten texts, re-using them with alterations on different occasions; many were later published.[8] He wrote them with great care, and they were delivered carefully as well, without any show of oratory; some were broadcast in later years (for example, one for Ascension Day in 1956, from the Oratory).

What distinguished his preaching was his ability to relate to his hearers - if visiting a particular place, he would make the effort to find out some historical or topographical detail and include this in the sermon. Something else that was distinctive was his use of the Bible, particularly the Old Testament, of which many Catholics knew little when compared to other Christians. Many of his most eloquent sermons are on the Eucharist; he preached every year for many years at Corpus Christi Church, Maiden Lane, on their feast of title; they illustrate how far the Mass was at the centre of his spiritual life. This is from one of the best known, 'The Window in the Wall'; he is talking about the voice at the window in Canticles (*Songs* 2:9): '…That voice at the window brings to my own mind a fancy which I have often had…in looking at the sacred Host enthroned in the monstrance. The fancy, I mean, that the glittering disc of whiteness which we see occupying that round opening is not reflecting the light of the candles in front of it, but is penetrated with a light of its own, a light not of this world, shining through it from behind, as if through a window, out-dazzling gold and candle flame with a more intense radiance…'

Knox and the literary converts

Knox's conversion happened at a time when many major figures in English literary and cultural life were committed Catholics, and most of them were converts, including G.K. Chesterton[9], Eric Gill, Compton Mackenzie, Graham Greene and Evelyn Waugh; one whom Knox got to know well was Hilaire Belloc.

His first book after his conversion was *A Spiritual Aeneid*, written primarily to explain to Anglicans why he had acted as he had. Also at this stage he collaborated in a 'spoof' edition of Horace, *Odes* book V; as Waugh puts it 'he was engaged in ephemeral writing which occupied part of his restless intelligence and supplemented his

salary.' He wrote a number of newspaper columns and
also a satire of contemporary biographies, *Memories of the
Future*, a book about King Henry VI, a diatribe against
Spiritualism, and *Sanctions: A Frivolity*. This last book is
a novel set in a house party where the guests discuss in a
Platonic manner questions such as the role of the state, the
ideal person, education and above all the sanctions for
deciding right and wrong. This suited the mood of the
times, the questioning which took place after the carnage
of the First World War. As in Knox's earlier Anglican
controversial books and pamphlets and his later apologetic
works, the underlying theme is the notion of authority.

Radio broadcasting in the early 1920s was in its
infancy. During his life Knox was sometimes sceptical
about its value; but he did often broadcast and his
broadcasts are often remembered[10] - particularly a hoax
broadcast during the General Strike at the beginning of
1926, 'Broadcasting from the Barricades'[11] It described,
among other things, a demonstration in Trafalgar Square
threatening to sack the National Gallery, led by an
organisation called the *National Movement for Abolishing
Theatre Queues*. Like other 20th century spoof
broadcasts, modelled on this one, it caused great anxiety
and the BBC was inundated with enquiries. The hoax was
widely attacked in the press - including *The Tablet*, at that
time seen as the mouthpiece of Cardinal Bourne. The
alarm, which seems extraordinary to us, shows how

unfamiliar people were with the new medium of communication and the atmosphere of fear following the Russian Revolution. Also in these years Knox started writing detective stories, which were very successful and usefully supplemented his income.

Back to Oxford

Chaplaincraft

One of Bishop Edmund Knox's 'last ditch' arguments against his son's conversion to Catholicism was that the Roman Catholic Church would not be able to use his talents - his great ability would be wasted. Among those who knew him in the early 1920s there would have been a feeling that this was turning out to be true, as he was simply a Latin teacher in what was then, even by Catholics, considered to be a minor public school. Knox himself never showed any resentment: his diffidence and genuine humility, and his deep loyalty to ecclesiastical authority, would never allow this to come to the surface. But after six years he was getting restless and there were painful dissensions with the school and college.

In July 1926, after considerable hesitations (and the earlier opposition of the cardinal) Knox was appointed Chaplain to Catholic students at Oxford University. This was the only official ecclesiastical post he ever held and the thirteen years he was in the office were the only period of his life when he lived in a place which could really be called his own home, as opposed to an institution or

someone else's home; and in many respects it is the
central period of his life. From 1867 until after the death
of Cardinal Henry Manning in 1892 Catholics had been
formally prohibited by the Holy See from going to Oxford
or Cambridge, because of dangers there to their faith;
when the ban was lifted, the setting up of chaplaincies in
both universities also entailed the provision of regular
'conferences' for undergraduates, to be given by the
chaplain or another priest, to counteract bad influences.
The chaplaincy, centred on an old building near St
Aldate's known as the 'Old Palace'[12] was not well-
endowed financially: one reason Knox wrote detective
novels at this period was to supplement its income. At this
time the university was almost entirely male (and the
chaplaincy certainly was: female students were meant to
go elsewhere) and far smaller than it is today - the
overwhelming majority of Knox's flock (in 1926 they
only numbered about 125 men; it had grown to about 170
by 1939) were from the Catholic public schools.

When he left the chaplaincy in 1939 Knox wrote a
long handbook for his successor, *The Whole Art of
Chaplaincraft*, which outlined in great detail the nature of
his ministry, together with the foibles of the part-Tudor
building which the chaplain occupied. Waugh in his
biography gives a fascinating account of this document
(never published) and its practical, down to earth
approach; unlike a priest in a parish or a school, Knox

had very little help for the running of things, apart from a housekeeper supplied by his friend Lady Lovat. This extract gives a flavour: 'The second-floor bedroom has been condemned by the delegacy [*the University body which had to approve student accommodation*] as unsuitable accommodation for an undergraduate; I have therefore been compelled to sleep in it myself.'

Pastoral ministry

The nature of Knox's pastoral ministry was very different from what he had done as chaplain at Trinity College before the war. While the chaplaincy provided three Sunday Masses, only two were really for the student population (one was for people from the town); here he was not an academic tutor or part of the university system; he depended on undergraduates making the effort to come to see him, and he facilitated this through an organised system of invitations to drinks parties and dinner: at his meals the only desert offered was bananas, a custom going back to his time at Trinity, as he maintained that the banana was an ideal food which could be eaten in any position and without the need of crockery or utensils. He was, of course, responsible for them in a different way; the young had changed since the heady years before the (1914 - 1918) war; and he himself was older. He made it a priority (apart from an hour in the afternoon when he walked round Christ Church meadow reading his Breviary) to be simply available in his room at the chaplaincy for casual callers. He also took undergraduates as lodgers. He carefully avoided any suggestion that he was there to win converts - he saw this as the concern of others. He fitted quickly back into the life of the university, being elected to dining rights at Trinity and becoming once again a regular speaker at the Oxford Union; in short, an Oxford 'character'.

The provision of Sunday Mass was obviously central to what the chaplaincy was about. In contrast to his Anglican days, Knox by this time had developed an aversion to elaborate ritual[13], his life being centred on the simplicity of Low Mass (he was also notoriously unmusical) and was openly relieved that in the university year the only slightly unusual ceremony which altered the regular pattern was the imposition of ashes on Ash Wednesday (he describes the annual search for a holy water vat and sprinkler); apart from confession, the other sacraments were seldom celebrated; he was helped by priests from the religious houses in Oxford, particularly Campion Hall (which was very near the Old Palace) and Blackfriars (a Dominican priest said the third Sunday Mass[14]).

Conferences

At the heart of his ministry were the 'conferences' referred to above: half-hour discourses given after the final Mass each Sunday in term time. Cardinal Bourne had made clear his view that they should form a continuous course of apologetic: Knox put this into practice by starting (in 1926) with the existence of God; the final conference at the end of three years, logically enough, was on the responsibilities of marriage, including Catholic teaching on birth control. While this had relevance for men about to leave Oxford, it was of course a 'rolling programme' with new students joining each year, so like all such courses it had drawbacks. After Knox left Oxford they were published in a collection entitled *In Soft Garments*. Like his other sermons, these are works of great charm and style, showing deep knowledge not only of the issues of the day but of the pressures facing undergraduates in the 1920s and 1930s.

This extract from the last one he gave as chaplain in 1939 gives a good flavour, showing both seriousness and gentle wit:

'It is just over forty years now, that Leo XIII first allowed Catholics to go up to Oxford and Cambridge. If he had foreseen the course of things, he would have said to them, "I send you forth as lambs in the midst of wolves." Wolves in sheep's clothing if you like; wolves in Old Etonian ties and so on, but wolves for all that; I mean, in the sense that their bewildered acquiescence in our modern materialism is an influence working for the labefaction of all sane principles. If he had seen you sitting here now, that great Pope would have wished you, I think, the gift of tenacity.'

What preoccupied Knox above all were dangers to the faith of his impressionable charges from the uncertainties of the 20s and 30s; all the time the message is clear: they should be faithful to the Church, receive Holy Communion more frequently, be able to explain their faith, and marry a Catholic girl.

The flowering of Knox's apologetic

Both the content and the style of the conferences are linked to the major works on Catholic apologetic which came from this period; Knox had time to write, as the Oxford University academic year occupies less than six months. Fr Walsh's recent study (see the section at the end of this booklet on further reading) gives the best overall picture of Knox as an apologist, but we can look at some of the best examples of what he wrote in his chaplaincy period.

The most renowned book was *The Belief of Catholics*[15], written originally in 1927. In the preface Knox gives a succinct description of what apologetics is about: 'This book...is an attempt to write constructive apologetic, to assert a claim; and if the specialist feels inclined, as doubtless he will, to button-hole me here and there with a demand for fuller explanations, I must offer him the discourtesy of hurrying on; there is no space for them.' A book of apologetics must not be too long, and it is not a work of standard theology; it exists *to assert a claim* - to state 'what I believe.'

One thing which perhaps surprises us is the context for the work to which Knox draws attention: distaste for religion, and continuing hostility towards the Catholic Church in particular. We are inclined to think that religion was far more secure in public life in 1927 than it is now; yet Knox was not the only person to feel that countless beliefs had been undermined in his own lifetime up to that point. Accommodations by the churches (which he had criticised as an Anglican) had not led to growth in congregations, quite the reverse: 'Dogmas may fly out at the window but congregations do not come in at the door.' By contrast, he shows that the only religious body experiencing sustained growth rather than decline is the Roman Catholic Church.

Sharp analysis

He is also blunt in his assessment of how far previously common moral standards have ceased to be so: 'Within the last fifty years an open challenge has been issued to traditional morality in matters concerning sex. A steady, ceaseless flow of literary propaganda has shaken the faith of our generation in the indissolubility of marriage, hitherto conceived as a principle of natural morality. Let anyone contrast "Jane Eyre" with the average modern novel, and he will see how far our thought has travelled. Fifty years ago, it was assumed, even in more or less free-thinking circles, that divorce was a disreputable subject, and that remarriage after divorce was a disqualification for respectable society. Today, such principles are maintained among Christians only with hesitation, among free-thinkers not at all.' He goes on to make the same point about artificial contraception.

His awareness, too, of abiding distrust of Catholicism and lack of understanding is also timely. In the years following the war, Catholics were perhaps inclined to think that they were fully accepted in national life. Knox describes the cabinet minister in 1914 who questioned whether there needed to be more Catholic army chaplains because Catholic soldiers could be ministered to by French priests: 'When it was pointed out to him that these priests would find some difficulty in hearing confessions, it proved that the Cabinet minister had assumed, all his life, that Catholics made their Confessions in Latin. One pictures those Irish troops, a Kennedy in every knapsack.'[16]

Faith and reason

Knox's priority in the book is to establish the correct relationship between faith and reason, attacking the widely held view among both Protestants and non-Christians that Catholics suspend or suppress the use of reason in relation to the claims of their religion, and the claim that Catholics simply accept all their beliefs on the strength of the Church's authority, and nothing else. He retorts that Catholics accept these doctrines not on the basis of authority but rather reason[17]: the existence and nature of God; his revelation in Christ; the broad outlines of Christ's life, death and Resurrection; his foundation of the Church; and the teaching authority of the Church. For Knox the problem is that Protestants see faith as a matter of personal experience or merely the will, whereas the Catholic Church has always taught that faith entails an act of intellectual assent. Moreover, non-Catholics have nothing to fall back on when historical criticism raises questions about the hitherto unquestioned authority of Scripture, hence the stampede, as he saw it, to abandon central Christian beliefs: 'For three centuries the inspired Bible had been a handy stick to beat Catholics with; then it broke in the hand that wielded it, and Protestantism flung it languidly aside.'

The genius of the work is the way in which Knox maintains a disciplined approach in his examination of the six beliefs referred to above. So, unusually in a book of Catholic apologetics, when he deals with revelation he invites his readers to consider the Old Testament and the history of the Jews in isolation, at first, from the New Testament; similarly when looking at the person of Christ he cites first Roman historical sources and later non-biblical Christian works, before looking at the New Testament; and when he does open the New Testament he starts with the Epistles and their picture of belief in Jesus' Resurrection - all before he examines the gospels. All this is designed to show the basis of belief in *rationality*, through looking at historical source-material.

Jesus in the Gospel

He applies the same rigorous technique to the claims of Jesus and the picture in the gospels. As Walsh explains: 'What is the evidence that might justify Jesus' claim? Knox suggests (1) the fulfilment of the Old Testament - not of specific texts but of the general expectation behind the prophetic literature; (2) the wisdom of Jesus' teaching; (3) his miracles; and (4) above all, his Resurrection. Concerning the last, Knox notes that Jesus expected to rise from the dead and that his tomb was in fact empty. The best natural explanation for this is that the disciples stole the body; but psychologically, it would have been difficult for this frightened group of followers to have staged such a deception and willingly embraced death for what they knew to be a fraud. Finally, they reported appearances of Jesus after his death. This evidence does not produce mathematical certainty, nor should it be expected to. Historical evidence can only be expected to remove reasonable doubts - and according to Knox, the Gospel records of Easter faith can do this.'

Authority

Following on from this, it is logical to expect Christ to have left a community to carry forward his work, and to teach with his authority; and such a community needs a focus of unity, the successor of St Peter: all this is believed on the basis of reason, not authority. But once that authority is accepted as being necessary, everything else falls into place; as Walsh puts it: 'Once the inductive conviction of the infallibility of the Church is made, her doctrines follow deductively. These doctrines cannot originate in reason, because they are revealed by God and must be accepted on divine authority. Among these doctrines are the Trinity, creation and Fall of first parents, redemption, Incarnation, Virgin Birth, the Church as the Body of Christ, the sacramental system, the Real Presence of Christ in the Eucharist, the Last Things. For Catholics, these are not simply a series of statements. Rather, they are a manifestation of the supernatural life that is part of the air Catholics breathe: "Faith knows what it does not experience. It is a conviction, not a consciousness, that the other world is close at hand."'

More writing

The Belief of Catholics was one of Knox's most popular and influential books. Other works which reflect the same apologetic theme from this time were *The Church on Earth* and *Caliban of Grub Street*. This was a mocking prod at a group of popular writers (Arthur Conan Doyle, Arnold Bennett and others) who had contributed 'symposia' published in the popular press attacking the claims of religion, in the years following the publication of H.G. Wells' *Outline of History*. Knox not only pokes fun at them, but dissects what passes for argument in their writings. As Waugh puts it: 'He sifts out the agnostics, the atheists and the cranks, the vaguely ethical and the vaguely immoral. There is no consistent ethos. This, he concludes, is modern thought outside the Catholic Church; not the most acute thought, but what the newspapers find most purchasable.' In *Broadcast Minds* he turned his attention to Julian Huxley's *Religion Without Revelation* and Bertrand Russell's *Conquest of Happiness*. Knox's concern is to refute the claim that Christians distrusted scientific enquiry.

This literary debate prompted the publication of letters between Knox and one of his critics, Sir Arnold Lunn, *Difficulties*. Lunn had earlier been more critically agnostic, but by this time was more positive about the Christian faith which meant that dialogue was more fruitful than it might have been. Lunn raises difficult historical questions such as the ministry of bad popes such as Alexander VI and the appalling actions of the Spanish Inquisition; Knox side-steps many of these. A year after book's publication Lunn was received into the Church by Knox. In all these writings Knox actually saw popular interest in religion as a sign of disbelief.

From 1929 Knox enjoyed a very good relationship with the Archbishop of Birmingham, Dr 'Tommy'

Williams; his contacts with his own ordinary, Cardinal
Bourne, were rather more distant, but this changed in
1935 with the succession to Westminster of Archbishop
Arthur Hinsley - this coincided with a radical alteration in
the ownership and editorship of *The Tablet*, for which
Knox henceforward became a regular contributor. In
1936 he was appointed a Domestic Prelate to Pope Pius
XI, carrying the title 'Monsignor.' Particularly in his
closing years at Oxford, he became more self-critical as
far as his pastoral abilities were concerned, and felt that
too many undergraduates were lapsing from the faith and
that he had been at Oxford long enough; he also
experienced bad health and his housekeeper died. He was
not the only Catholic 'Oxford character' of these years;
others who were very influential included the philosopher
Fr Martin D'Arcy SJ (a close friend of Knox) and the
social thinker Fr Charles Plater. But in the last two years
of his time at Oxford his life began to be transformed by
his friendship with a convert whom he had instructed,
Daphne, Lady Acton. He became part of the Actons'
social circle and spent vacations at their country house at
Aldenham, in Shropshire; he also wrote a delightful novel
as his parting tribute, as it turned out, to his university,
Let Dons Delight.

Translation of the Bible

Knox's restlessness and the more imaginative view of his talents from Cardinal Hinsley meant that by the beginning of 1938 he was definitely ready for a move; not, however, to be President of St Edmund's, where he had taught nearly twenty years before, which the Cardinal offered him, almost certainly the first step to becoming a bishop. Knox was horrified by the idea and declined it; what he wanted to do was to produce a new translation of the Bible, and the Actons were happy to install him as their chaplain at Aldenham for him to have the necessary seclusion to do so.

Catholics and the Bible

For over three centuries the Bible used by English Catholics had been the Douay-Rheims version, substantially revised in the 18th century by Bishop Richard Challoner. It has great beauty and was influential on the Authorised Version, but its almost literal closeness to the Latin of the Vulgate, the Church's official text of the Scriptures, made it very hard to understand by the 20th century - particularly the letters of St Paul. There had been a consensus since the 1850s that a new translation, not a revision, was necessary, and a version had appeared in

America which had never been adopted here, the
Baltimore Bible. At the end of 1938 the hierarchy
officially commissioned Knox to translate first of all the
New Testament; in these early years of translating work he
was also engaged in writing new translations of Latin
hymns for the *Westminster Hymnal* and an abortive project
to revise the *Manual of Church Prayers*.

Knox's preaching and writing drew on his deep
knowledge of the Bible, not a knowledge shared by most
Catholics (particularly with regard to the Old Testament,
which at this time was seldom read at Mass), even the
clergy. He wrote later: 'When I used to go round
preaching a good deal, and would ask the Parish Priest for
a Bible to verify my text from, there was generally an
ominous pause of twenty minutes or so before he returned,
banging the leaves of the sacred volume and visibly
blowing on the top. The new wine of the gospel, you felt,
was kept in strangely cobwebby bottles.' Knox had been
brought up in an Evangelical household where the Bible
was read aloud in the family every day; he wanted
Catholics to develop the same familiarity with the Word of
God, reading it at home and understanding it - by this time
too the Sunday readings at Mass were read in English
after they had been read in Latin. There was, as Speaight
puts it, a 'gap which Ronald Knox was destined to fill
between Protestants who knew the Bible at the expense of
the Church and the Catholics who hardly knew it at all.'

Framework

Catholics nowadays are used to versions of the Bible which are frequently shared, by and large, with other Christians, such as the *Jerusalem Bible* and the Catholic editions of the *Revised Standard Version*; moreover these are direct translations of the Hebrew and Greek originals. Until the Second Vatican Council the first feature would have been unthinkable, and the second considered rather suspect: the Latin Vulgate, St Jerome's translation from the originals, was the Church's official text and translations were still expected to be from that, not from the originals. Knox, with his reverence for authority, was happy with this; but made sure that he consulted the originals (teaching himself Hebrew very quickly) and recorded variant readings. There is unending controversy about what style of English the Scriptures should follow. He aimed to write in what he called 'timeless English', diction that would not age, or would age only slowly. A man as literate as Knox, and as steeped as he was in the Authorised Version, would inevitably write in fairly traditional English (he uses the 'thou' form of the second person). Knox's translation has great charm and beauty; literary critics suggest that the epistles of St Paul are the most successful.

His misfortune was that the two characteristics of Catholic Biblical translation referred to above had evaporated within a decade of the final publication of the whole Bible in 1956. By the mid-1960s Catholics were encouraged to produce translations directly from the Hebrew or the Greek so versions which were based on the Vulgate were simply out of date; so the Knox Bible is seldom used today, although it was used for three Biblical books in the 1974 English *Divine Office* (Wisdom, Galatians, and parts of Romans). Furthermore, the text of the Vulgate itself has been significantly revised and a new edition was published as the normative version in 1979, and is the one used in the second Latin editions of the Mass lectionary and the Office. It is also the case that the history of the Bible's publication was long and occasionally marked by disagreements with some members of the hierarchy (together with those whom Knox was expected to consult) who hesitated over giving official sanction to what Knox produced. Knox was first and foremost a priest: he accepted these vicissitudes in a spirit of humility and reverence for episcopal authority, and they should not be exaggerated[18]; after 1950 he would not accept the financial payments due to him.

The New Testament was published with official authorisation from the bishops in October 1945; his translation of the Old Testament received an *imprimatur* 'for private use' in 1949; the final version of the whole Bible, fully authorised, came out in November 1955, by which time he had also published a New Testament commentary[19]. For all the problems and subsequent developments Knox's translation of the Bible remains his most significant achievement; other modern versions are the work of committees, serviced by large teams of researchers - the Knox Bible is all his own work, and all done within one room.

It is hard to find one example of the grace of Knox's translation, but this captures some of his style:

'I may speak with every tongue that men and angels use; yet, if I lack charity, I am no better than echoing bronze, or the clash of cymbals. I may have powers of prophecy, no secret hidden from me, no knowledge too deep for me; I may have utter faith, so that I can move mountains; yet if I lack charity, I count for nothing. I may give away all that I have, to feed the poor; I may give myself up to be burnt at the stake; if I lack charity, it goes for nothing. Charity is patient, is kind; charity feels no envy; charity is never perverse or proud, never insolent; does not claim its rights, cannot be provoked, does not brood over an injury; takes no pleasure in wrong-doing, but rejoices at the victory of truth; sustains, believes, hopes, endures, to the last.'[20]

Ministry to school children

The Bible was penned in one room because he had much less space at Aldenham than he had anticipated in 1938; once again a key development in his life was the outbreak of world war. In 1939 all over England schools were evacuated from the cities to the countryside, and the Convent School of the Assumption in Kensington was sent to Aldenham - eventually 55 girls, 15 nuns, 3 lay teachers and a lay matron spent the whole war there[21]. Knox had expected quiet seclusion for his translation; now, not only was there a war on, with the attendant deprivations, but a school was to take over most of the country house where he was staying. It was agreed that he would act as chaplain to the school.

There is no evidence that the girls' presence slowed down the translation (they were strictly instructed not to disturb him), but the encounter worked very well and his ministry to them was unexpectedly fruitful. Many of them became friends at whose weddings in later years he preached or presided; the girls combined reverence for him with real affection. We can see at close hand what the relationship was like from the '*Slow Motion*' books referred to in the introduction above (among the most popular books he ever wrote).

As in other settings Knox was able to relate to the world-view of his listeners and explain the truths of the Christian faith at their level. Again we see the concerns of apologetic; again, as in the sermons he had delivered at Corpus Christi, Maiden Lane, we see his deep devotion to the Mass, the heart of his life. While *The Mass in Slow Motion* was obviously written to accompany the earlier form of the Roman Rite, many of its insights are timeless.

Here he is talking about the point in the Eucharistic prayer just before the consecration: 'What happens if the priest falls down dead at this point? The answer is that you say one Hail Mary for my soul and go back to breakfast; there is nothing special to be done about it; I mean about the Mass. For all intents and purposes it hasn't started yet. Three minutes later, when the Consecration has happened, if the priest who is celebrating the Mass falls dead or is taken gravely ill, any other priest who can be got hold of must finish off the Mass, even if he isn't fasting; even if he is under ecclesiastical discipline and is forbidden in the ordinary way to celebrated any Sacrament at all.' Children the world over are excited by hypothetical events like this; Knox uses a very simple situation to illustrate an important point.

There is so much warmth in this extract from the final sermon: 'You won't find it easy to remember me; you will grow into your new surroundings very soon, and they will be different surroundings. Only one thing is never different; the Holy Mass. Every now and then, perhaps, some gesture, some trick of manner about the priest who serves your chapel there will bring back to you memories of Aldenham; you will find yourself saying, "Do you remember how old What's-his-name always used to blow his nose during the server's Confiteor?"… In Christ we are all one; the sacred Host is the focus in which our rays meet, regardless of time and space. Only we must keep true to him; only we must go on saying that prayer the priest says before his Communion, asking that though he is separated from everything else he may never be separated from our Blessed Lord: *A te numquam, a te numquam, a te numquam separari permittas.*' ('May I never, never, never be permitted to be separated from you')

God and the Atom

The Second World War affected Knox differently from the first; he did not have to scour the lists of dead to look for his friends, but his basic personal needs (tobacco, razors) were more affected by shortages and his travels to preach in different parts of the country were hampered by disruptions to railway timetables (of which he had expert knowledge). But one event which brought the whole war to an end hit him more than any other: 'At a moment when it seemed as if all our capacity for surprise were already exhausted, one day last August, we opened our paper to find that we were wrong... A Japanese town, rather more populous than Southampton, had suddenly ceased to exist.'[22]

After the bombing of Hiroshima on 6th August 1945 Knox waited for an authoritative statement from the hierarchy; he carried on waiting after the bombing of Nagasaki, and indeed, although Pope Pius XII unequivocally condemned the bombings, shamefully, there was not to be a clear condemnation of nuclear weapons from the Catholic bishops in this country for over sixty years[23]. In the end he wrote a letter to *The Times* pleading for the Allies not to do it again, but on the way to the post-box he heard that Japan had surrendered, so he decided not to post it. He wrote *God and the Atom* in the space of a few weeks, 'one of Knox's most important books...also one of his least successful.' It is one of the most original critiques of the bombing and the intention to use nuclear weapons which has remained a cornerstone of many countries' foreign policies ever since; it was, in Speaight's words 'the most prophetic reaction to Hiroshima to have been uttered in any language.'

Steeped in St Paul's theology, Knox analyzes what happened in the light of the three theological virtues of faith, hope and charity: all three had been struck a blow by the bombing. Throughout his apologetic writing he had sought to demonstrate the existence of God from order in creation: the splitting of the atom appears to threaten this by showing an indeterminate nature, or anarchy, at the heart of things, questioning all our ideas of reality, common sense, metaphysics and physics. This was the chill of doubt.

Hope was threatened by the chill of despair, which he examines in the chapter, 'The Fading of a Dream.' The wars of the twentieth century had shattered belief in progress, in the betterment of the world; in 1945, 'Never has the world given thanks for peace with such a deep sense of disillusionment.' Looking at the offence against charity, he writes: 'Theologically speaking, my thesis is that it would have been a more perfect thing not to bomb Hiroshima. Or, if I must needs talk the language of common life, let me dig up a phrase from an almost forgotten, but not altogether unregretted past, and say that bombing Hiroshima was not cricket.' Only Knox could have written that. It would have been better to have made a 'generous gesture'; while not indifferent to the possible loss of lives on the Allied side, he shows that it would have been better to drop the bomb in a deserted place to demonstrate its power without killing anyone.

Prophetic insights

One of the worst things that will happen, he predicts, as a result of the bomb is the abandonment of self-restraint - people will become more self-assertive and selfish, because the dropping of the bomb showed such a lack of restraint: 'I suspect, then, that those minds which are now in the making will be a bad surface for receiving the polish of altruism. The appeal of religion will come to them as a thing alien from their own unconscious prepossession... Will they not tell us, the men of the new generation, "We are atom-children; do not be surprised if we turn out worthy of our breed?"'

But all is not gloom: the Christian faith offers alternatives. Indeterminacy in the world of nature makes the mystery of creation deeper; as far as hope is concerned, Christians now have a special responsibility to build *true hope*. There have been many false starts, shattered now by the reality of war: 'We faced war, and went through with it...and at the moment of victory, a sign appeared in heaven; not the comforting Labarum of the Milvian Bridge, but the bright, evil cloud that hung over Hiroshima. In this sign we were to conquer.' In the chapter dealing with the recovery of charity Knox suggests that religion has the responsibility of binding people together, of integrating people's lives, of resisting the movement towards what we would call now 'atomisation': '...If you make a man less of a citizen he tends to become more of an individual. Nature takes its revenge; if he cannot find elbow-room in his civic environment, he is all the more eager to make the most of his own personality; a slave by accident of external circumstances, he will be ruler in the narrow kingdom of his soul.'

There is much more in *God and the Atom*; but it is clear that it is a work of disturbing prophetic force. The abandonment of restraint ushered in, or at least hastened, by the dropping of the bomb has further weakened the influence of religion; combined with rising prosperity (a distant dream in 1945) this has led to a weakened sense of society, of community - people are more turned in on themselves. Finally, although international co-operation has brought sustained peace between nations in some parts of the world (such as most of Europe), unrestrained violence still has a strong hold. As popes and bishops have pointed out with increasing fervour since 1945, states which hold nuclear weapons and make clear their intention to use them have no credibility as keepers of world peace; the false sign is still in the sky.[24] Christians have been slow to take up Knox's challenge in *God and the Atom*, and Knox was saddened that the book provoked very little reaction or criticism. In a way it was too early - before people were fully aware of the effects of the bombing, long before any movement against the bomb; and Britain was drained and war-weary.

Closing years

Mells village

Knox's friends the Actons decided that they would be more successful farmers in Southern Rhodesia (Zimbabwe) than in Shropshire and prepared to leave Aldenham, so he had to find somewhere else to live.[25] He moved to the village of Mells in Somerset, to stay in the home of Katherine Asquith (the widow of Raymond Asquith, son of the First World War Prime Minister H. H. Asquith) whom he had received into the Church, and her son, the Earl of Oxford and Asquith.[26]

In his first years at Mells he was engaged in completing his translation of the Old Testament. He also wrote about the art of translation itself, in *On Englishing the Bible*. With the misunderstandings past, he was honoured at a special lunch in London when the whole Bible was published in November 1955 where he made a speech of great wit, comparing himself, as 'author' of the Knox Bible, with others who had given their names to objects such as Hoover and Sandwich. He also denounced revisions of translations: "Will somebody suggest, fifty years hence, 'It is time that the Knox Bible was revised, and brought up to date?' Then, oh, then, gentlemen, I have a charge to leave with you. If any suggestion is made, then let the youngest person who is present today rise in his bath-chair and cry out, 'No! The whole point and protest of the Knox Bible was that it is a mistake, this continual revising and refurbishing of existing Scripture translations, this continual cutting down of father's pants to fit Willie. To revise the Knox Bible would be a treachery to the memory of its translator. If it is dated, then let it be scrapped; let somebody else sit down and undertake the whole task afresh, in a style of his own, and with a treatment of his own; let him give us, not a pale rehash of the Knox Bible, but a new Bible, and a better!'"

In 1949 he published his favourite book, on which he had been working for twenty years, *Enthusiasm*. This was a study of differing religious movements in Christian history characterised by a belief in direct divine inspiration, such as Jansenism and Methodism. Backed up by extraordinarily detailed research it has a unique place among Knox's books as a work of 'pure' research, rather than a work written for some special purpose, and it attracted favourable academic comment. While he approaches the subject matter from the standpoint of Catholic orthodoxy, he is not unsympathetic to figures such as John Wesley and saves some of his harshest words for enemies of the movements he examines, such as Bossuet ('an odious fellow').

His abilities did win external recognition by this stage. During the war he had been elected an honorary Fellow of Trinity College, and later to the 'Old Brotherhood' of the English Secular Clergy. In 1952 he was made a 'higher grade' of Monsignor, a Protonotary Apostolic *ad Instar Participantium*[27]: he made his only visit to Rome as a Catholic[28] and had an audience of Pope Pius XII, with whom he apparently discussed the Loch Ness monster; there are suggestions that some thought he should be a bishop or a cardinal, both honours which he would have viewed with dread. Among those whose friendship he valued after he went to Somerset were the novelist Anthony Powell (whose books he found 'too difficult') and the war poet Siegfried Sassoon, who became a Catholic partly owing to his influence; in 1953 he made a long visit to Africa, visiting Southern Rhodesia and Zanzibar.

In 1956 he wrote a new translation of St Thérèse of Lisieux's autobiography, *The Story of a Soul*. Like others he felt that devotion to this remarkable woman[29] had been surrounded with sickly sentimentality[30]; he once remarked of her 'When Catholics get hold of a good thing, they do their best to spoil it.' It was a paradoxical relationship, as he wrote: 'I have a superstition that she [St Thérèse] was asked in Heaven whom she'd like to as her translator, and replied "Ronald Knox - he'll mind my style so terribly, and the great thing is always to do something you don't like.' In these years collections of sermons and retreat addresses were published.

He also started work on a new work on apologetics. What he wrote was published by Waugh after his death under the title *Proving God: A New Apologetic*. As Walsh points out there are signs in what he did write that his approach to apologetics was changing with advancing age; he makes it clear that the old are more tolerant than the young: 'The world is no longer divided into angels who agree and devils who disagree with him... Experience has softened the hard edges of his affirmations. If I may use words in a grossly unphilosophical sense, what he demands now is not so much truth as reality.' Therefore revelation that comes from God has to be presented in a particular way: 'Thus the presentation of the divine fact to the human mind calls for persuasion; and if you would persuade, you must have some knowledge of how people's minds work, of the ideals which move them and the prejudices which enchain them. Experience is no longer to be despised, and even an old man's book may be worth the writing.' It is perhaps not too fanciful to suggest that this shift to some extent anticipates some of the insights of the Second Vatican Council.

The road to death

Knox's father had lived well into his eighties, so at the age of 68 there was no reason to think that he did not have some years of work ahead of him; but he was unwell at the end of 1956 and by the spring of the next year it was clear that he had cancer of the liver and had only months to live[31].

He said Mass for the last time in June 1957. That month he was due to give an important public lecture in Oxford, the Romanes lecture, which was entitled *On English Translation*. It was given in the Sheldonian Theatre on 11th June; he was very weak and many knew that he had cancer and was dying; he illustrated a point during the lecture with William Johnson Cory's rendition of a Greek epigram:

'They told me, Heraclitus, they told me you were dead,
They brought me bitter news to hear,
and bitter tears to shed;
I wept when I remembered how often you and I
Had tired the sun with talking and sent him down the sky.
And now that thou art lying, my dear old Carian guest,
A handful of grey ashes, long, long ago at rest,
Still are thy pleasant voices, they nightingales, awake;
For Death, he taketh all away, but them he cannot take.'

Many hearers were in tears as he made this farewell to Oxford. He went from there to 10 Downing Street to stay with the Prime Minister, his old friend Harold Macmillan, who had arranged for his doctor, Sir Horace Evans, to give a second opinion on his condition; this confirmed the earlier diagnosis of terminal cancer. When Macmillan saw him on his train back to Mells he said, 'Well, Ronnie, I hope you have a comfortable journey', to which Knox replied 'It's a long journey I'm going on.'[31a]

He declined very rapidly after that. He received Holy Communion for the last time on 11th August; on the 20th he was asked if he would like extracts read to him from the New Testament. He declined and said, 'Awfully jolly of you to suggest it, though' which were his last words. He died on the 24th.

He was buried in the churchyard at Mells, after a funeral Mass in Westminster Cathedral, presided over by Archbishop Godfrey; the preacher was Knox's old friend Fr Martin D'Arcy SJ.

Knox's achievements

There are at least two pitfalls for us as we assess Ronald Knox's abiding importance; the first is to dismiss him as the creature of a bye-gone age which came to an end with the Second Vatican Council: the Catholic world in which he lived, the air he breathed (to use his own image) have changed so much that he has little to say at the beginning of the twenty-first century. His own self-deprecating modesty would probably warm to such a view. The second is related - a tendency to be nostalgic about that world and see him as a champion of some possible return to its certainties, and its liturgy. Because much of his writing and preaching is so firmly centred on the way in which Mass was celebrated seventy years ago, it is perhaps easy to restrict his insights to that form of the Roman rite, and assume that he would, were he alive now, avoid the 1970 Missal like the plague.[32]

Both these positions are damaging to the Church and false to his memory; it is clear that his genius and message make him an important figure in the mainstream of Catholic life.

There are at least four areas of his writing and preaching which give him continued importance.

Apologetics

The first, as I indicated in the introduction, is the art of apologetic. Knox was preoccupied with the need to enable all Catholics to give a reasoned account of their faith within a society increasingly distant from Christian belief and practice. The tendencies he identified eighty years ago have accelerated, both in terms of religious practice itself and any sense of shared, rational moral standards. When he wrote *The Belief of Catholics* the wider acceptability of divorce was a sign that the rot had set in; he would have reacted with bewilderment (at first) to the Human Fertilisation and Embryology bill of this year 2008. The challenges posed by legislation like this make it even more urgent that we are able to explain our convictions in rational terms, so his concerns and method are relevant.

Atomic Bomb

Linked to this would be a second area: his critique of the dropping of the atomic bombs in 1945 and the effects of this on wider society. He was saddened that *God and the Atom* had so little effect: and yet it is clearly one of his most prophetic works: not only in terms of how far the act itself threatened Christian principles of faith, hope and charity, but because he was so right to identify how it has 'atomised' society and helped to make people not only more violent, but more turned in on themselves. The weakness of civil communities, and indeed of political life in many places, can be traced to the bombing of Hiroshima and the ethos of cynicism which it has engendered. What he wrote should also strengthen Christian witness against nuclear weapons.

The Bible

Catholics see the Mass as being in two parts, the Liturgy of the Word and the Liturgy of the Eucharist, and my last two areas of importance correspond to these. Although Knox's translation of the Bible faded quickly from the central role it played in Catholic life in the the1950s, his concern - that Catholics should be as familiar with the Word of God as other Christians - has begun to be realised. While there are many reasons for this, his translation and work is partly responsible for this, and he deserves some of the credit: the priest he describes blowing the dust off a Bible is no longer to be found.

Spirituality

Knox's Eucharistic spirituality, the food for his own soul, remains deeply valuable for all of us. The Church is engaged in a constant process of deepening our understanding of the Eucharistic mystery, drawing on all the riches of our tradition; we can easily read a book about the 'old rite', allowing for things that have changed and realising that it is in essentials the same Mass, rooted in the Church's teachings and God's love for us. In current disputes about liturgy, two extreme tendencies do so much damage - the one which claims that nothing which antedates the post-conciliar reforms is of value; the other which says that the Mass was destroyed by what happened. Knox's writings help us to reject these false views and embrace both continuity and development: with just a little bit of effort we can relate to his writings about the Mass. For those of us who are priests, these words from *The Priestly Life* about the Divine Office surely speak to us whatever book we are using, and whatever language it is in: 'Jesus Christ, our High Priest, is going to offer himself in the Holy Mass, using you as his tool - his dull, uncomprehending tool; you will offer yourself, motionless, into his hands... You take up the well-thumbed breviary; and arrange the tattered markers in it. You know well what your office is going to mean; a verse or two read with some sense of what the meaning is about, but alas, with no unction; then a long rumination on your own affairs, starting off at a wide tangent; then the bell that rings in your memory and recalls you to a sense of what you are doing; always the same. A parrot, you feel, would do it as well. To be sure, but at least you can take upon yourselves the duties of God's parrot; the beasts, too, praise God.'

In all these matters Knox speaks to us because of his ability to understand our concerns; if we can relate to our parents' or grandparents' generations, we can relate to him, and thank God for his grace and eloquence.

A feature of his spirituality is the feeling, never far away, that heaven is always closer to us than we think;

this vision of heaven and the saints (full of so many characteristics of his writing), from a sermon preached to schoolboys in 1950, and is a good note on which to end:

'… Let us remember that the curtains of heaven are transparent curtains. Not in the sense that you or I can look in; ah, if only we could! What a world of good it would do us! No, but the saints can look out; they can see you and me still ploughing our way through the mud and darkness of this earthly existence, feeling our way with difficulty and falling, every now and again, into the ditch. And they can help us; not only because the light of their example shines down on us, and makes it easier, sometimes, to see what we ought to do. They can help us with their prayers, strong prayers, wise prayers, when ours are so feeble and so blind. When you look out on a November evening, and see the sky so studded with stars, think of those innumerable saints in heaven, all ready to help you…'

Further reading

Ronald Knox was a very prolific writer, who towards the end of his life said that he no longer recalled how much he had written and that he doubted whether the recording angel would know either; even now some of his writings have not been published; most are out of print, and some are to be found in more than one place. For a full list see *www.ronaldknoxsociety.com* and the appendix to Waugh's biography.

The Ronald Knox Society of North America offers an invaluable resource for further study; a number of Knox's writings can be downloaded from the website referred to above.

The authoritative biography remains this official one written by Evelyn Waugh shortly after his death (*The Life of the Right Reverend Monsignor Ronald Knox*, London: Chapman and Hall, 1959). Although the author's well-known snobbery is seldom far from the surface (you get the impression he never quite got over not having been at either Eton or Shrewsbury himself) this is more than outweighed by his affectionate sympathy for his subject and the detail of his account of Knox's life and writings, drawing on private papers to which he had access as his literary executor and the book is beautifully written. However, Waugh's picture of the relationship between Knox and the bishops in relation to the translation of the Bible is unfair and oversimplified, particularly with regard to Archbishop Amigo: see on this Michael Clifton, *Amigo: Friend of the Poor* (Leominster: Fowler Wright, 1987), pp.120-126, which records more of the correspondence than Waugh does.

Waugh predicts in his introduction that weightier books would be published on Knox's spirituality and theology, but this has not really happened; while there have been some valuable studies there has been no work comparable to Waugh's; Tom Corbishley SJ *Ronald Knox the Priest* (London: Sheed and Ward 1964) and Robert Speaight, *Ronald Knox the Writer* (London: Sheed and Ward 1966; in America the two books were published together) are two early studies worth reading. Another more recent book of great value was written by Knox's niece, Penelope Fitzgerald - *The Knox Brothers* (London: Macmillan, 1977). Her father was Ronald's oldest brother Eddie and the work portrays well the relationship between the four brothers and their fascinating lives.

The most important recent book is by Fr Milton Walsh, *Ronald Knox as Apologist: Wit, Laughter and the Popish Creed* (San Francisco: Ignatius 2007). As well as giving a good biographical summary it looks at specific aspects of Knox's apologetics. Walsh has had access to unpublished 'conferences' among the papers kept at Mells where Knox died.

Many of Knox's more popular works are often to be found in second-hand bookshops. Of those which have been reprinted in recent years are in England Knox's own favourite work, *Enthusiasm* (London: Collins: 1987) and in the USA *The Belief of Catholics, The Church on Earth, Captive Flames, Pastoral and Occasional Sermons, The Hidden Stream* and his translation of *The Imitation of Christ*.

Endnotes

[1] 'The prevailing attitude...was one of heavy disagreement with a number of things which the speaker had not said.' Dr Williams, in the speech on 11th February 2008 (for the full text see *www.archbishopofcanterbury.org*) was referring to the tumultuous reaction to his remarks about Shari'a law. Knox was referring to a discussion at the Newman Society in Oxford in the 1930s. Unfortunately the portrayal of Knox in Brenton's play is inaccurate.

[2] On the brothers see Penelope Fitzgerald, *The Knox Brothers* (London: Macmillan, 1977).

[3] See Trevor Meriol and Leonie Caldecott, *John Henry Newman* (CTS B 655).

[4] *Ronald Knox as Apologist* (San Francisco: Ignatius Press, 2007), pp. 29ff.

[5] This word was used negatively by the movement's critics; Knox is glorying in the accusation.

[6] Knox's friend Fr Maurice Child applied for a chaplaincy posting. He was turned down when asked how he would minister to a dying soldier. He said that we would hear his confession and give him absolution, whereas the correct answer was 'Give him a cigarette and take any last message he may have for his family.' (Evelyn Waugh, *The Life of the Right Reverend Monsignor Ronald Knox* [London: Chapman and Hall, 1959] p. 135)

[7] Macmillan, who was Prime Minister in 1959, is referred to as 'C' in the earlier part of Waugh's biography, as he is by Knox in *A Spiritual Aeneid*.

[8] *Pastoral Sermons and Occasional Sermons* (London: Dropmore Press 1949). One of his sermons, for the feast day of St Edward the Confessor (12th October), also appears in *The Divine Office* (volume III).

[9] Knox admired Chesterton greatly and played a significant part in his conversion to Catholicism in 1922. At this time Chesterton wrote this quatrain:

> 'Mary of Holyrood may smile indeed,
> Knowing what grim historic shade it shocks
> To see wit, laughter and the Popish creed
> Cluster and sparkle in the name of Knox.'

[10] A collection of CDs of them can be purchased via the Ronald Knox Society website.

[11] The script was later printed in *Essays in Satire* as 'A Forgotten Interlude' (London: Sheed and Ward 1954) pp. 187ff.

[12] Knox was fascinated by the history of the building, put up by the first and last Catholic Bishop of Oxford, who held office under Henry VIII, Edward VI and Mary: 'I picture the old man striding up and down this very room where I said office this morning, trying to adapt himself to the altered conditions of 1553 - saying goodbye for the nonce to *Dearly Beloved Brethren*, banging off the dust of five years from his neglected breviary and starting out again on *Aperi Domine*. What a retrospect was his. He had seen Wolsey fall, and Cromwell, and now Cranmer was going the same way. He had seen the monasteries dissolved and shared in their spoils, and now the loot was in danger. He had taken the Oath of Supremacy and now he saw the Supreme Head of the Church of England declare she was nothing of the sort. The times were out of joint; surely it was not Robert King's province to set them right... I confess I go to bed the more courageously for the knowledge that my predecessor made a good end.' (*The Universe*, 10th December 1926, quoted in Waugh, *op.cit.*, pp. 211-2.)

[13] He valued the beauty of ceremonial when it pointed to a doctrinal truth, although (partly because he was so unmusical) he felt rather alarmed by having to perform rituals himself ('It is a long time since I had to sing High Mass, and when I did, the only thought I can remember entertaining was a vivid hope that I might die before we got to the Preface.' [*The Mass in Slow Motion* p. x]). He certainly did not value ceremonial for its own sake: 'Mystification, mummery for mummery's sake, exasperates me beyond speech; and I have never been able to understand my countrymen's partiality for Masonic and quasi-Masonic ritual.' (*The Belief of Catholics* [2nd. Ed., London: Sheed and Ward, 1939], p. 32)

[14] 'The bother is that the Dominicans insist on saying an odd kind of Mass, which needs a server accustomed to the rite' *The Whole Art*, quoted by Waugh, *op.cit.*, p. 217.

[15] It was first published in 1927 and Knox made slight alterations for the second edition in 1939, which is used here; a fourth edition was published in 1953 which is the one used by Walsh in his book.

[16] 'Kennedy' refers to the standard Latin primer used in schools for most of the 20th century.

[17] This contrasts with the reasons for his conversion - for him, authority had been the key issue.

[18] M. Clifton, *Amigo: Friend of the Poor* (Leominster: Fowler Wright, 1987), pp. 120-126, shows that Waugh presents the Bishop of Southwark and his attitude to Knox in an unfair light, and records more of the correspondence; the picture is more complicated than Waugh allows.

[19] His Lenten conferences preached in 1950, *St Paul's Gospel*, were published by CTS and have recently been reprinted (Sc 87).

[20] 1 Corinthians 13:1-7.

[21] The word 'evacuee' entered the English language, so Knox could not resist a Latin quip: *'"Eva, cooee", pulsus Pardiso dixit Adamus; Echo responsum reddidit "Evacuee"'.*

(*In Three Tongues*, ed. L. Eyres [London: Chapman and Hall, 1959], quoted in Speaight, op.cit., p. 29. (*"Eva, cooee!" said Adam after he had been ejected from Paradise. The echo gave an answer, "Evacuee"*)

[22] *God and the Atom* (London: Sheed and Ward, 1945). Before the book was published extracts appeared in *The Tablet*. Elsewhere in the world one of the few other Catholic voices condemning the bombings was the American Dorothy Day: see Ashley Beck, *Dorothy Day* (CTS B 705), pp. 45ff., with notes. Pius XII called the bombing a 'crime against God and man… This war provides a catastrophic conclusion. Incredibly this destructive weapon remains as a temptation for posterity, which, we know by bitter experience, leans so little from history.' (*L'Osservatore Romano* 7th August 1945)

[23] The clearest statement has been the call by the Bishops' Conference of England and Wales for the decommissioning of all British nuclear weapons on 21st November 2006 (see *www.catholicchurch.org.uk*; follow the links for press releases in 2006).

[24] See most recently Pope Benedict XVI's World Peace Day message for 2006, to be found in *www.vatican.va*, follow the links for World Peace Day messages.

[25] When he left the country house he had to close up the chapel which he had used; a few years before he described what this process would involve (removing the altar stone, etc.) to Evelyn Waugh who used this to depict such as scene in his novel *Brideshead Revisited*.

[26] Ironically, in view of Prime Minister Asquith's well-known anti-Catholicism (see *Benedict XV*, note 17, pp. 72-3). Lord Oxford had lodged at the Old Palace while at Oxford.

[27] Knox said that this honour entitled him to wear a mitre once a year, something of which he did not avail himself (he could in fact have done so more often); the syllables of his new honour fascinated him and he wrote some verses about it all in the style of Gilbert and Sullivan.

[28] Knox once said: 'He who travels in the barque of St Peter had better not look too closely into the engine room' in Fitzgerald, *op.cit*., p. 258; this is often quoted.

[29] See CTS B 204, by Knox's long-standing friend, fellow convert and successor in the Oxford chaplaincy Msgr Vernon Johnson.

[30] Another who attempted to correct this was Dorothy Day, who wrote a biography of St Thérèse; see *Dorothy Day* pp. 61-62 and notes.

[31] Two of his brothers, Dilwyn and Wilfred, had died of cancer by this time.

[31a] Walsh, *op.cit*., p. 64.

[32] Waugh claims that Knox was unhappy with the liturgical changes introduced in the 1950s such as the revision of the Holy Week rites and small introductions of the vernacular. However, in *The Mass in Slow Motion* Knox makes a number of suggestions which anticipated later reforms, such as the transformation of the Secret prayer into the Prayer over the Offerings, said out loud. One of his constant concerns was the ignorance of the Old Testament among most Catholics, so it is inconceivable that he would not have welcomed the vast increase in Old Testament readings both on Sundays and weekdays in the 1969 Lectionary, and the two- and three-year cycles which increased so much the amount of Scripture read at Mass.